Original title:
Love's Lingering Language

Copyright © 2024 Swan Charm
All rights reserved.

Author: Kätriin Kaldaru
ISBN HARDBACK: 978-9916-86-653-5
ISBN PAPERBACK: 978-9916-86-654-2
ISBN EBOOK: 978-9916-86-655-9

## **Whispers of the Heart**

In quiet corners where shadows play,
Soft sighs linger, guiding the way.
A melody hums in the still of night,
Two souls entwined, hand in hand, a sweet sight.

Each heartbeat whispers, secrets unfold,
Stories of love in silence retold.
With every glance, a promise is shared,
In the hush of the moment, two hearts laid bare.

## **Echoes of Unspoken Affection**

In the spaces where words seem to fade,
A glimmer of hope in each gesture displayed.
Unseen connections pulse like a song,
In the rhythm of longing, where we both belong.

Time slows down in the warmth of your gaze,
Every heartbeat a dance, in delicate maze.
An echo of laughter lingers so near,
In whispers of longing, love's truth is sincere.

## The Poetry of Silent Glances

In the stillness, our eyes gently meet,
We weave our stories, a tapestry sweet.
Words left unspoken, yet so full of grace,
In the silence, we find a familiar space.

A flicker of light in a crowded room,
Two souls collide, dispelling the gloom.
With every heartbeat, a verse takes flight,
In the poetry crafted from day into night.

## **Beneath the Veil of Touch**

Fingers brush softly, a spark ignites,
Beneath tender veils, the world feels right.
In the warmth of your palm, I find my peace,
Each fleeting moment, a sweet release.

The language of touch, so gentle, so pure,
In every caress, our spirits assure.
Entwined in a dance that words cannot tell,
Beneath the soft veil, love whispers its spell.

## **Whispers in the Hallway**

Softly they murmur, shadows creep,
Secrets in silence, promises deep.
Footsteps that linger, hearts intertwine,
In the stillness, your soul calls mine.

Echoes of laughter, memories glow,
Whispers of love that ebb and flow.
Time stands still, with each gentle sigh,
In this quiet dance, forever we lie.

## **Echoes of Affection**

In the breeze, I hear your name,
Each whispered word is a gentle flame.
Through the night, your touch remains,
In dreams we meet, breaking all chains.

Stars align in the sky so vast,
Every heartbeat brings forth the past.
Moments cherished, never to fade,
In the echoes of love, we've always stayed.

## The Subtle Art of Yearning

In the quiet of dusk, my heart takes flight,
Searching for you in the fading light.
Each heartbeat whispers, longing so true,
Like petals drifting, I'm drawn to you.

The canvas of night, painted with dreams,
In silent shadows, nothing's as it seems.
With every glance, I feel the flame,
In this subtle art, I breathe your name.

## Silent Sonnet of the Heart

Between the words, a silence sings,
A melody wrapped in tender springs.
The pause of moments, soft and sweet,
In the quiet places, our souls meet.

Crimson blush of the twilight hue,
Shapes of secrets, known to just a few.
Together we weave a tapestry fine,
In the silent sonnet, your heart is mine.

## Caresses That Often Speak

Soft fingers trace the dreams we weave,
In silence, our hearts learn to believe.
A gentle touch, a fleeting glance,
In tender moments, we find our dance.

The shadows sway in quiet light,
Each heartbeat whispers through the night.
Your laughter blooms like spring's first flower,
In every caress, we find our power.

With every brush of skin on skin,
Old scars fade, and new tales begin.
The warmth of you, a soothing balm,
In your embrace, I find my calm.

Mysteries wrapped in soft delight,
We paint the stars with whispered flight.
In secret corners, we unfold,
The stories only we have told.

So, let the world around us fade,
In gentle hues our love is laid.
Through caresses that often speak,
We find the solace that we seek.

## **Whispered Tales of Us**

Underneath the silver moon,
We share our dreams, softly croon.
With every whisper, hearts ignite,
In whispered tales, we find our light.

The breeze carries our secrets far,
Beneath the glow of a guiding star.
With every sigh, a new chapter penned,
In the language of love, we transcend.

Moments linger, time stretches thin,
In your gaze, I see where we've been.
Each laugh a melody, sweet and rare,
In the echoes of night, we lay bare.

Our hands entwined, the world can't see,
The magic woven between you and me.
With stories whispered on the breeze,
We bask in love's quiet ease.

So hold this moment, let it last,
For in each tale, our hearts are cast.
In whispered tales of soft embrace,
We find our timeless, sacred space.

## **The Universe between Heartbeats**

In the silence between our breaths,
Lies a universe, no words confess.
Galaxies dance in each heartbeat's sway,
In the rhythm of love, we find our way.

Stars collide in the depths of night,
Every pulse a beacon, shining bright.
With every glance, we create the whole,
Two souls merging to become one goal.

Infinite dreams in a fleeting touch,
Time stands still, oh, it means so much.
The cosmos whisper secrets true,
In the space between me and you.

Planets spin in this fragile dance,
Each heartbeat echoes a bold romance.
In this universe, we freely roam,
Every heartbeat brings us home.

So let's explore what time can't find,
In every moment, our hearts aligned.
For in the universe that unfolds,
Between our heartbeats, love's story is told.

**Echoes of Handwritten Promises**

In ink, our dreams are scribed,
Each word a whispered vow,
Time may wear the pages thin,
But echoes linger somehow.


A letter sealed with gentle care,
In shadows of a restless night,
Our hopes take flight on paper wings,
Illuminated by soft light.


The scent of parchment, warm and sweet,
Carries tales of love and fear,
Handwritten secrets come alive,
In every stroke, we hold you near.


Ink stains mark our joyful tears,
Through hardships, we still stand tall,
Each promise whispered, written clear,
A testament through it all.


We scatter notes like autumn leaves,
Across the paths we chose to roam,
Though distance stretches far and wide,
Those echoes lead our hearts back home.

## The Soft Footprints of Connection


On sandy shores, two paths entwine,
Each footprint left, a memory,
The waves will kiss the lines away,
Yet we remain in harmony.


In quiet woods, where whispers breathe,
The rustling leaves tell tales of us,
Nature cradles our shared breath,
A bond that time cannot discuss.


The softest touch, a fleeting glance,
Like petals falling from the tree,
In every moment, silence speaks,
A language felt, but seldom free.


Through crowded rooms, our eyes will meet,
A spark ignites, a flicker bright,
With every shared and stolen smile,
We find our way back to the light.


So hand in hand, we'll leave our mark,
A tapestry of laughter sewn,
The footprints fade, but hearts alive,
Will carry love wherever grown.

**Secret Choreography of Hearts**

In stillness, we find our rhythm,
A dance beneath the moon's embrace,
With every glance, our souls align,
Moving in a sacred space.


Unspoken words float in the air,
A melody soft, yet profound,
The sway of bodies, gentle touch,
In silence, our hearts resound.


Twirling shadows cast by lantern light,
We weave our path through night's ballet,
While stars above wink in delight,
Witness to our hidden play.


Each heartbeat thumps a steady beat,
Guiding us through the unseen dance,
A cautious step, then leaping joy,
Each brush ignites a second chance.


And when the dawn begins to creep,
The world awaits our secret art,
With every step, we leave a trace,
The choreography of the heart.

## **Impressions Left by Soft Eyes**

In softest gaze, the world unfolds,
A myriad of tales untold,
Through gentle pools of liquid light,
We find the warmth against the cold.


Each fleeting glance holds galaxies,
A window to the soul within,
Reflections dance on the surface,
Whispering where love has been.


With every blink, a story weaves,
The laughter, sorrow, dreams long lost,
In the silence, a truth revealed,
The soft eyes show what's worth the cost.


We trace the lines of etched emotion,
Sketching dreams in every stare,
The weight of memories gathers close,
A delicate tapestry laid bare.


Time may blur the vision clear,
But in the depths, we see the prize,
For in the softest gaze, we find,
The lasting impressions of our skies.

## Symbols of Solace

In the quiet of the night,
Stars echo whispers of hope.
Moonlight dances on the sea,
Guiding souls to gently cope.

Soft petals in the breeze,
Nature speaks in silent tones.
A warm hug can ease the pain,
Healing hearts, mending homes.

The sound of rain on the roof,
Each drop is a tender kiss.
Bringing peace, a sweet reprieve,
In its rhythm, we find bliss.

A familiar scent in the air,
Reminds us of days gone by.
In nostalgia, we find strength,
A soft smile, a gentle sigh.

As the sun breaks the dawn's hold,
New beginnings gently stir.
In symbols of solace found,
We discover who we were.

# The Radiance of Mutual Understanding

In shared glances, love ignites,
Words unsaid softly speak.
Hearts collide in sacred space,
Where silence holds the weak.

Through laughter and through tears,
We navigate this maze.
A knowing touch, a kindred soul,
In warmth, our spirit plays.

Time suspends in fleeting moments,
Where trust begins to bloom.
Like golden rays, we intertwine,
In shadows, we find room.

Unraveled threads, we weave together,
A tapestry of grace.
In every thread of understanding,
A masterpiece we trace.

As dawn brings light to the world,
Our hearts beat in the same.
In the radiance of kindness,
We discover love's true name.

## Reverberations of the Unsaid

In silence, echoes persist,
Words unspoken fill the air.
In every pause, a longing grows,
A whispered ache to share.

The weight of thoughts, like shadows cast,
Dance where no one can see.
Each heartbeat knits a story,
Of what could never be.

In fleeting glances we confide,
A language that feels true.
In the distance of our hearts,
An uncharted rendezvous.

Soft sighs melt into the night,
Yearning flows like a stream.
In the quiet of the moment,
We chase an elusive dream.

As time weaves its intricate threads,
Reverberations play their part.
In the silence we embrace,
We find the echoes of the heart.

## Fragments of Affection

In scattered pieces, love remains,
A jigsaw of shared delight.
In stolen moments, laughter sings,
Through shadows into light.

Tiny notes left on the fridge,
Sweet reminders of our tune.
In every glance, in every sigh,
Affection fills the room.

Memories flutter like leaves,
Colors vibrant, hues so bright.
Every fragment tells a tale,
Of love's unfathomable might.

Through photographs and cherished gifts,
Our journey's woven tight.
In the fragments of affection,
Love walks with us each night.

As seasons shift and time unfolds,
Each piece adds to our song.
In life's puzzle, found in parts,
Together, we belong.

## The Melodies of Affectionate Silence

In shadows, whispers twine like vines,
The silence sings in soft refrains.
Hearts converse where words fall short,
In quietude, love finds its port.

Stars flicker in the velvet night,
Each twinkle holds a shared delight.
Hands entwined, no need for sound,
In silence, our true selves are found.

The world fades, just we remain,
In gentle peace, we know no pain.
Each breath a note, a pulse, a rhyme,
Together, we flow in perfect time.

Like echoes of a distant song,
In this stillness, we both belong.
A symphony without a score,
In silence, we are evermore.

So let us treasure this sweet space,
Where love exists without a trace.
In melodies of silence deep,
Our hearts will sing, our souls will leap.

## **Vows Without Words**

Beneath the stars, our glances weave,
Promises made, no need to grieve.
A touch can speak what lips won't say,
In silence, love finds its own way.

Two hearts aligned beneath the moon,
In every pause, the softest tune.
Eyes like poets, writing fate,
In every glance, our souls translate.

With each heartbeat, a vow is cast,
In quiet moments, futures vast.
The universe listens in our hush,
In stillness, there is a gentle rush.

We write our story without a pen,
In the spaces where we begin again.
A world unveiled in silent trust,
These unspoken vows, forever just.

So may our love be ever loud,
In whispered tones, proud and unbowed.
Through depths of silence, we are bound,
In vows without words, true love is found.

## Surreal Stanzas of Togetherness

In dreamlike hues, our spirits dance,
With every glance, a second chance.
A world that swirls in colors bright,
Together, we paint the endless night.

Time bends gently in our embrace,
Unfolding moments, a sacred space.
With every heartbeat, we redefine,
Reality blurs, so intertwined.

Floating through realms of sheer delight,
A waltz of laughter, pure as light.
In stanzas woven soft and sweet,
Together, our verses make us complete.

The surreal whispers secrets low,
In shadows cast, our passions glow.
Each story told in silent grace,
Together, we find our rightful place.

In this dreamscape, forever roam,
Where the heart finds its true home.
A tapestry of love unfurled,
In surreal stanzas, we shape our world.

## **Echoes of Shared Dreams**

In twilight's hue, our visions blend,
Two souls entwined, begin to mend.
In echoes soft, our laughter rings,
Together, we reign in what love brings.

The dawn awakens dreams untold,
In every sigh, a future bold.
We chase the stars, hand in hand,
In shared dreams, together we stand.

Moments stretch beyond the dawn,
In unity, we carry on.
With every heartbeat, hopes ignite,
In echoes bright, we find new light.

Through valleys deep, and mountains high,
We craft our world, just you and I.
In dreams we've stitched with care and grace,
Echoes linger in every space.

For in our hearts, the vision grows,
A tapestry of love that glows.
Together we dance, our spirits soar,
In echoes of shared dreams, evermore.

## **Between the Lines of Our Souls**

In the shadows where we meet,
Words linger, bittersweet.
Silent whispers weave a thread,
In between all that is said.

Hidden glances tell the tale,
A soft touch, a gentle trail.
Hearts converse without a sound,
In these spaces, love is found.

Every pause holds sacred grace,
Moments stilled in time and space.
Intertwined, we softly sway,
Between the lines, we find our way.

Fleeting thoughts brush past the skin,
The quiet hum, where dreams begin.
In the silence, we can see,
The language of you and me.

So let us dance beyond the words,
In hidden realms, where hope is stirred.
With every heartbeat, soft and true,
We speak the lines that bind us two.

## **Where Silence Blooms**

In gardens where the quiet grows,
Soft petals hide in gentle flows.
The air is thick with unspoken dreams,
Where silence blooms and softly beams.

A hush surrounds the vibrant green,
In every leaf, a life unseen.
Moments linger, still and sweet,
In the dance of hearts that beat.

Whispers drift through fragrant air,
As two souls join, unaware.
In this realm, the world recedes,
And silence nurtures hidden seeds.

With every sigh, a blossom breaks,
In the quiet, our heart takes.
Together, planted side by side,
Where silence blooms, love must abide.

Each pause becomes a fragrant pause,
In the garden of our cause.
Let's cherish every soundless space,
Where silence blooms, we find our place.

## Hushed Notes of Togetherness

Underneath the starlit dome,
Hushed notes guide us gently home.
With every heartbeat, sweet refrain,
Together, we embrace the rain.

In the softest light, we stand,
Bound together, hand in hand.
Every gesture, rich in grace,
With whispers filling empty space.

The symphony of silent dreams,
Echoes in our sleepy themes.
In lullabies of dusk, we find,
The melody that's intertwined.

Through tender glances, love is shown,
In quiet moments, we have grown.
Each pause, a note that sings of two,
In hushed togetherness, it's true.

So let us weave this serenade,
In gentle hues, our hearts displayed.
Forever wrapped in softest song,
In hushed notes, where we belong.

## The Tapestry of Shared Silences

Threads of stillness intertwine,
In the weave of you and mine.
A tapestry of muted hues,
In every moment, we infuse.

Each pause a stitch, a careful art,
Binding softly, heart to heart.
Together in the quiet frame,
Where silence speaks, not all the same.

The fabric holds our whispered dreams,
In woven light, our essence beams.
Colors blend in soft embrace,
In shared silence, find our place.

With every touch, a thread is spun,
In the loom of love, we are one.
Every breath a seamless line,
In the tapestry, you're solely mine.

So let us craft this sacred weave,
In silent spaces, we believe.
A masterpiece of hearts aligned,
In the tapestry of love, we find.

## Beneath the Surface of Words

In whispers soft, the secrets hide,
Beneath the noise, they slip and glide.
A fragile dance of thought and sound,
Where truth and silence intertwine around.

Each syllable a wave that flows,
Through currents deep where no one knows.
The echoes linger, faint yet clear,
In hidden depths, we hold what's dear.

A tapestry of feelings spun,
In every pause, a world begun.
Beneath the surface, treasures gleam,
In the spaces where we dream.

The language spoken in the night,
Finds roots in shadows, fears, and light.
With every heartbeat, words ignite,
To weave a bond, ever so tight.

So listen close to what's not said,
In every glance, the paths we tread.
For beneath the surface of each phrase,
Lies a universe that gently sways.

## Heartbeats in Shared Spaces

In crowded rooms, we find our calm,
Where heartbeats dance, a soothing balm.
A rhythm shared, no words required,
In silent moments, souls are inspired.

The brush of hands, a fleeting fate,
A whispered smile, we do not rate.
In breaths exchanged, connection glows,
A bond of life that gently flows.

Through laughter bright and tears that blend,
In shared spaces, we transcend.
With every heartbeat, time stands still,
And in that pause, we learn to feel.

The universe in a single glance,
In crowded spaces, hearts will dance.
No barriers can hold us tight,
When love ignites the softest light.

So let our heartbeats intertwine,
In shared spaces, oh so fine.
For in the echo of this sound,
A deeper truth is always found.

**The Veiled Language of Togetherness**

In silence rich, a story's spun,
The veiled words speak, yet not in fun.
A glance, a sigh, the air is thick,
With meanings layered, subtle, and quick.

The gentle brush of shoulder and arm,
Conveys a warmth, a tranquil charm.
Each moment laced with unspoken dreams,
A dance of souls, or so it seems.

We navigate these hidden ties,
With every laugh, the truth complies.
In the spaces where our spirits play,
The language blooms, the veils give way.

From whispered thoughts to silent smiles,
Togetherness spans defying miles.
In the quiet, we find our voice,
In the togetherness, we rejoice.

So let us speak in veils and shades,
In every laugh, our bond cascades.
Through this veiled language, I see you,
In every heartbeat, all feels true.

## Tones of Unhidden Yearning

In twilight's glow, the shadows lean,
Yearning whispers shape the unseen.
With every glance, desires bloom,
In tones that linger, dispelling gloom.

The nightingale sings a secret tune,
In every note, our hearts attune.
A symphony of dreams takes flight,
In echoes deep, we chase the night.

From distant hills to oceans wide,
Yearning pulls, we cannot hide.
Each tender tone, a thread we weave,
In the fabric of the love we believe.

Though silence often fills the air,
In every pause, you know I care.
As stars above begin to glow,
These tones of yearning softly flow.

So let us dance in this embrace,
In unhidden tones, we find our place.
For in this music of the heart,
Yearning sings, never apart.

## **Echoing Hearts in Silent Rooms**

In quiet spaces, whispers play,
Where thoughts collide and drift away.
Each heartbeat echoes, soft and low,
Resonating feelings only we know.

Shadows flicker on the wall,
Memories wrapped in a gentle call.
Time stands still as silence reclaims,
The rhythm of love in whispered names.

Thoughts dance lightly on the breeze,
Carried softly through rustling leaves.
In peaceful corners, we reside,
With echoing hearts, forever tied.

The pulse of night, the depth of sleep,
In hidden chambers, secrets keep.
Each breath a muse, each sigh a song,
In silent rooms, where we belong.

Through quiet dreams, our spirits soar,
Hand in hand, we seek for more.
With every heartbeat, worlds are spun,
In echoing hearts, we are as one.

## A Tale Told in Glances

A fleeting look, a gentle gaze,
In crowded rooms, your eyes amaze.
Stories woven in silent threads,
Communicating all that's unsaid.

With every glance, a spark ignites,
Unspoken wonders break through the nights.
Two souls dance on a whispered tune,
Crafting a tale 'neath the silver moon.

In hurried moments, we find a way,
Through soft exchanges that long to stay.
A language formed in subtle smiles,
Telling our journey across the miles.

Each fluttering moment, a treasured spark,
While hearts entwine in the gathering dark.
With every heartbeat, more unfolds,
In a tale of glances, a story told.

So let our eyes speak evermore,
Of dreams and hopes we both adore.
In quiet reverie, it starts to dance,
A lasting love in a single glance.

## **Shadows of Sweetness**

In twilight's embrace, shadows grow,
Beneath the stars, where soft winds blow.
Whispers linger in the withered leaves,
Carried on dreams that the heart believes.

Raindrops glisten on gentle trees,
Echoing laughter, carried by breeze.
Moments sweet, like honeyed dew,
In shadows of daylight, I find you.

The night unfolds its velvet cloak,
With every breath, new dreams provoke.
Sweetness lingers in the air,
Binding us close, a tender pair.

In hidden corners, secrets bloom,
With laughter shared, dispelling gloom.
Hand in hand, we walk this night,
Bathed in the glow of soft starlight.

For in these shadows, love does thrive,
In the sweetest whispers, we come alive.
Bound by the moon's gentle embrace,
In shadows of sweetness, we find our place.

## **Heartstrings in Harmony**

In every note, our spirits blend,
With heartstrings pulled, we transcend.
Melodies wrap us like a shawl,
Guiding us gently, through rise and fall.

The music swells, a soft refrain,
Echoing dreams, like summer rain.
In perfect rhythm, our souls collide,
In harmony's arms, we'll forever abide.

With tender chords that make us whole,
Each strum reveals the longing soul.
A symphony born from whispered sighs,
Where love transforms and never dies.

Together we sway, in perfect tune,
Under the light of the silver moon.
Every moment sings a sweet embrace,
Each heartbeat played at a gentle pace.

In this concert of two beating hearts,
Love's melody flows and never departs.
Bound by the music, forever we thrive,
With heartstrings in harmony, we come alive.

## **Conversations Amidst the Stars**

Whispers carried on cosmic winds,
Dreams shared beneath the bright starlit sky.
Hearts converse where silence begins,
Hope unveiled with each twinkling cry.

Celestial bodies dance with grace,
Each spark a secret, a wish anew.
In this vast, enchanted space,
Voices echo, tender and true.

Galaxies swirling, a breathtaking sight,
We weave stories, like threads of light.
Lost in the beauty of the night,
Our words drift, floating in flight.

A moment captured, eternity's rhyme,
Every glance, a promise to keep.
In this vastness, we defy time,
Conversations linger, softly deep.

## **The Soft Bristle of Ears**

Gentle whispers brush like soft paint,
Curiosity blooms in hidden ways.
Childhood secrets, innocent and quaint,
Echoes of laughter fill our days.

The world shares tales, some joyous, some sad,
Innocence captured in moments so rare.
Listening patiently, never too bad,
Life's chapters unfold with tender care.

Soft bristles tickle, a delicate dance,
Each word received with warmth and grace.
In every silence, we find our chance,
To connect deeply, a shared embrace.

Through laughter and sorrow, we fortify trust,
Nature whispers secrets, old and revered.
In subtle exchanges, we find what is just,
The beauty of ears that have truly heard.

## **Threads of Emotion Woven in Time**

Moments stitched like a tapestry bright,
Every thread tells a story of old.
Emotions spill in the softest light,
Memories linger, both timid and bold.

Joy dances lightly, grief bows its head,
An interplay of laughter and tears.
In each tiny fiber, a heartbeat is fed,
The fabric of life woven through fears.

Time is a loom, spinning fast and slow,
Winding our paths, frayed edges align.
Through each twist and turn, we learn how to grow,
Threads of emotion, intricately bind.

Colors of love and sorrow entwine,
A canvas painted with hopes and dreams.
In every stitch, a heartbeat we find,
Life is a journey, unraveling seams.

## The Art of Unvoiced Promises

In the silence, we speak without words,
Promises linger in glances, a spark.
A touch conveys what the heart ensures,
In the quiet, we light up the dark.

With every heartbeat, intentions unfold,
Unvoiced promises dance in the air.
In moments held close, the truth is told,
Trust intertwines in the love that we share.

Eyes meet softly, a story unspooled,
In the stillness, we craft our own fate.
Against the noise, our hearts remain ruled,
In unspoken vows, we cultivate.

Life's sweetest secrets, whispered with grace,
Language of souls that need no translation.
In the silent embrace, we find our place,
Artistry woven in gentle elation.

## **Intimate Nuances of Connection**

In the quiet space between our words,
Silent whispers softly dance.
Every glance a secret heard,
In shadows, we find our chance.

Time flows like a gentle stream,
Carving paths where moments meet.
In laughter, we weave a dream,
A language felt beneath our feet.

Through shared smiles, our hearts align,
Painting stories, vivid and bright.
In the echo of your sigh,
I find solace in the night.

Glimmers linger in your gaze,
Each pause a testament to trust.
In the maze of tender ways,
Our spirits rise, they gently must.

A bond forged from unspoken ties,
In moments wrapped, we dare to dive.
Intimate nuances, no disguise,
In this connection, we arrive.

## The Unwritten Letters

In the quiet of the night,
Words dance like fireflies bright.
Thoughts penned in shadows deep,
Unwritten letters, secrets to keep.

Pages blank, yet stories flow,
From heart to heart, they softly go.
In silence, a longing grows,
For words that tilt and rise like prose.

Ink drips softly, time suspended,
Moments cherished, not yet ended.
What we lack in spoken grace,
We find within this sacred space.

Fingers trace the air with care,
Letters linger everywhere.
In dreams we find a paper trail,
A love letter that will prevail.

Unwritten lines connect our souls,
A symphony the heart consoles.
In the stillness, we reflect,
These letters deep, we shall protect.

## Murmurs of the Soul

In the stillness of the night,
Murmurs rise like softest light.
Each breath a tale, softly told,
In whispers warm, our hearts unfold.

Echoes linger, gentle tunes,
Carried by the silver moons.
In the depths of quiet sighs,
The soul reveals where silence lies.

Hushed confessions wrap around,
In the darkness, solace found.
Every heartbeat, a rhythm divine,
In the shadows, our spirits shine.

Here we dwell, where secrets speak,
In the silence, we are weak.
Yet in vulnerability, we heal,
Our essence shared, an unvoiced seal.

Murmurs of love, soft and true,
Every moment, me and you.
In these echoes, a tapestry,
Stitched together, eternally.

## The Lilt of Longing

Underneath the starry night,
Echoes of our hearts take flight.
In the distance, a soft refrain,
The lilt of longing calls your name.

Crickets sing their timeless song,
As shadows dance, we both belong.
In the hush of twilight's gaze,
Our souls entwined in gentle ways.

Every sigh a melody,
A whispered dream, just you and me.
In longing swift, our fingers trace,
A story etched, a warm embrace.

And though the night may steal our time,
In fleeting moments, love will climb.
A lilt that rises, brave and bold,
An echo of wishes yet untold.

Together in this yearning space,
We find our rhythm, our own place.
In the dance of heartbeats near,
The lilt of longing draws us here.

## **Our Hearts in Unison**

In the quiet moments shared,
Two souls dance as one,
Drifting softly through the air,
A melody begun.

With every whispered secret,
A bond begins to form,
Heartbeats race in rhythm,
A refuge from the storm.

Underneath the starlit sky,
Promises softly made,
Hand in hand, we wander by,
In love's eternal shade.

Each laugh is an echo sweet,
Joining in perfect time,
Two hearts in sync, a heartbeat,
An endless, tender chime.

As dawn breaks in golden light,
Our dreams begin to soar,
In the warmth of shared delight,
Forever wanting more.

## The Currency of Warm Glances

In a crowded room, we stand,
Eyes meeting, hearts collide,
Unspoken words, hand in hand,
A silent joy we can't hide.

Each glance is worth a thousand tales,
A price above all gold,
With every look, our spirit sails,
A warmth that never grows cold.

Caught in the web of fleeting time,
Moments woven tight,
Your gaze, it feels like poetry,
A soft and glowing light.

Stolen glances shared between,
The world fades to a blur,
In your eyes, my heart is seen,
No words need to occur.

In this currency, we trust,
A bond that comes alive,
With every warm glance, it's just,
A reason to revive.

## Whimsy in the Midnight Hour

Underneath the velvet sky,
With stars that play and tease,
Awake, we let our laughter fly,
And dance with gentle breeze.

Midnight whispers call our names,
A shimmer in the night,
In our hearts, we spark wild flames,
In shadows bathed in light.

Every dream a playful whim,
As moonlit paths unfold,
Together on this joyous limb,
Our stories to be told.

Moments weaving through the dark,
With stardust in our veins,
We chase the dreams, ignite the spark,
As life unfolds in chains.

With every tick of midnight's clock,
We breathe the magic in,
In the realms where wonders mock,
Our hearts begin to spin.

## **Written in the Language of Touch**

With every brush of our fingers,
A silent story speaks,
In the softness, warmth lingers,
Where connection truly peaks.

The world fades, it's just us,
In the silence, we ignite,
Hand in hand, a sacred trust,
Our bond feels oh so right.

Each caress, a line unwritten,
A sonnet made of skin,
In every heartbeat, we are smitten,
Letting sweet love begin.

In this dance, we share our essence,
Bodies swaying, hearts unfold,
Each moment holds pure presence,
A tale of love retold.

Written in this language rare,
A love that's bold and true,
In the warmth of touch, we share,
A world made just for two.

## **The Rhythm of Heartbeats**

In shadows whispers softly play,
A pulse of night, a gentle sway.
Two souls entwined in tender grace,
As heartbeats dance in quiet space.

The world around falls still and fades,
While time dissolves in secret glades.
With every beat, a story told,
Of love that's warm and never cold.

Beneath the moon's soft silver light,
Our dreams converge, take flight at night.
Each thump a promise, soft and sweet,
Where life and love in rhythm meet.

In perfect sync, we find our way,
As heartbeats weave a bright array.
With every sigh that leaves our lips,
The melody of love's eclipse.

So let the night by silence mark,
The pressing pulse, a fleeting spark.
For in this sacred, quiet bliss,
We find the joy in every kiss.

## **Unfurling Emotions**

Like petals open to the sun,
Our feelings bloom, two hearts as one.
Each layer peels, revealing truth,
A tapestry of love and youth.

With laughter soft and tears that gleam,
We navigate this winding dream.
The colors swirl, a vibrant hue,
A canvas painted just for two.

In silence shared, our spirits soar,
A language rich, no need for more.
Beneath the weight of every sigh,
Our hearts unlock, they learn to fly.

Through storms we face, and sunshine bright,
Our journey weaves with pure delight.
Each moment shared, a thread unwinds,
We cherish all the love that binds.

So let us dance in sweet embrace,
As feelings flow, we find our place.
With every heartbeat, joy unfolds,
Unfurling emotions, love's strong hold.

## **The Poetry of Proximity**

When you are near, the world feels right,
A simple glance ignites the night.
In every touch, a spark ignites,
Creating beauty in our sights.

With whispered words like velvet air,
Each moment shared, beyond compare.
Your laughter lingers in the space,
A melody, a sweet embrace.

The inches close yet miles apart,
In every beat, I feel your heart.
A quiet grace, the warmth we share,
The poetry of love laid bare.

In crowded rooms or quiet halls,
In every glance, my spirit calls.
Together woven, hand in hand,
In proximity, love's steady stand.

So let us revel in this dance,
With every look, a daring chance.
The poetry of us combined,
In every breath, our souls aligned.

## **Soft Murmurs at Midnight**

The clock strikes twelve, a hush descends,
In whispered words, the evening bends.
Soft murmurs float like dreams on air,
As secrets shared ignite the flare.

Beneath the stars, a canvas wide,
Our hearts entwined, we cannot hide.
Each gentle breath, a tender beat,
With quiet love, we find our seat.

In shadows deep, the night unfolds,
With every sigh, a story told.
Time drips slowly, moments freeze,
In midnight's glow, our souls appease.

As crickets sing their lullabies,
We drift away in soft replies.
With every word, a star ignites,
Soft murmurs dance in moonlit nights.

So let us breathe in twilight's shroud,
In whispers shared, our hearts are proud.
Beneath the heavens, close and true,
Soft murmurs at midnight, just me and you.

## A Canvas of Quiet Devotion

In the hush of morning light,
Brushstrokes of love take flight.
Whispers of dreams gently weave,
Each moment, a treasure to believe.

Palette rich with hues of grace,
Softly, our hearts find a place.
Canvas stretched, a silent art,
Devotion paints each beating heart.

As twilight beckons the stars,
We find ourselves, near and far.
Color shades of laughter bloom,
Filling the canvas of our room.

Each sigh a stroke, each glance bright,
We share colors both dark and light.
In this quiet, we remain,
Forever bound, love's sweet refrain.

Our brush moves with tender care,
Creating memories we both share.
On this canvas, pure devotion,
Life's beauty flows—an endless ocean.

## **Freckles of Affection**

Like stars upon a summer's face,
Freckles dance in warm embrace.
Each spot a story to unfold,
In the sunlight, love is bold.

These little marks, so sweet and rare,
Remind us of the moments we share.
Laughter caught in tender glow,
Freckles tell of love we know.

Chasing shadows, running free,
Underneath the old oak tree.
Nature's art, a playful sign,
Every freckle feels like mine.

In the dusk, their shimmer fades,
Yet still, in hearts, the warmth invades.
Soft reminders of what's true,
Freckles lie in love with you.

In every touch, a spark ignites,
Freckles echo sweet delights.
With every glance, affection's song,
In this garden, we belong.

**When Touch Becomes a Dialogue**

In a silence beyond the words,
Fingers speak like gentle birds.
Every brush ignites a flame,
A language deep, never the same.

Eyes meet in an unspoken trance,
Touching hearts, a timeless dance.
Each caress tells tales untold,
In this grasp, love's truth unfolds.

Skin to skin, we share the night,
A communion, pure and bright.
In warm whispers, secrets shared,
Our tender bond, a love declared.

Moments linger, soft and slow,
In this dialogue, emotions flow.
Each touch a note in the air,
Melodies only we can share.

As dawn breaks with its golden hue,
Our hands entwined, we start anew.
Through every pulse, our hearts abide,
In this symphony, side by side.

## The Pulse of Hidden Sentiments

Beneath the surface, gentle beats,
A rhythm pulsing, love repeats.
Hidden words in silence play,
Emotions drawn in shades of gray.

Heartbeats whisper tales unspoken,
In languid grace, bonds unbroken.
Every glance a secret shared,
In the quiet, souls bared.

Between the lines, the truth awaits,
A language spun that love creates.
Subtle signs, a tender glance,
Within the silence, our dance.

In shadows deep, the heart confides,
Where vulnerabilities abide.
Each pulse resounds with sweet intent,
In this space, our hearts are lent.

As twilight wraps the world in blue,
We find the words waiting for cue.
With every beat, love's echoes call,
In hidden realms, we find it all.

## The Language Between Breaths

Whispers swirl in softest air,
Each breath a story we both share.
In silence speaks what words can't find,
A bond unbroken, soul entwined.

Threads of sighs, a gentle thread,
Connecting hearts, where words have fled.
The pauses linger, sweet and bright,
In every pause, a spark of light.

Moments hang like dew on leaves,
A tender sigh that gently weaves.
In breaths that dance beneath the skin,
The truth is felt, where love begins.

In every heartbeat, deep and true,
The language whispers, me and you.
A symphony of heartbeats blend,
Breaths composing, never end.

Together in this sacred space,
We find our truth, our warm embrace.
In every silence, we are found,
The language shared, without a sound.

## **Intimacy's Gentle Cadence**

Each touch a note, a soft refrain,
Melodies that dance like summer rain.
In tender glances, pulses rise,
A symphony beneath the skies.

With whispered truths upon the skin,
A rhythm flows, where love begins.
In quiet corners, hearts align,
The music fades, yet still we shine.

The warmth of hands, a soft embrace,
In silence found, we hold our place.
With every heartbeat, every sigh,
In intimacy, we learn to fly.

The gentle cadence of our day,
With laughter bright, we chase away.
In every moment, close we stay,
Intimacy's song, our own ballet.

Through seasons change, this tune remains,
In love's sweet dance, there are no chains.
Together woven, strong and bold,
In every note, our story told.

## **Unseen Bonds of the Spirit**

In shadows deep, connection grows,
A silent thread where feeling flows.
The heart knows paths, though eyes can't see,
In every breath, a tapestry.

Through whispered thoughts and dreams we share,
The spirit dances, light as air.
Unseen yet felt, these ties embrace,
A sacred bond, a timeless grace.

In moments still, we find the way,
To weave our souls in bright array.
The light within, though dimly cast,
A glow that lingers, strong and vast.

In unity, we rise and fall,
In whispered truths, we hear the call.
Bonds of the spirit, fierce and kind,
In each connection, love defined.

Through journeys wide, we brave the storm,
In every heart, a hidden form.
Together we stand, hand in hand,
In unseen bonds, forever planned.

## **The Dance of Furtive Shadows**

In twilight's grasp, shadows arise,
A dance unfolds beneath the skies.
With every shift, a secret kept,
In whispered moves, the night is swept.

The moonlight glimmers on the floor,
Where hidden hearts yearn to explore.
With every curve, the silence sings,
In shadows, love takes gentle wings.

The waltz of whispers light as air,
In fleeting glances, moments rare.
Each step a story, softly told,
In furtive glances, hearts unfold.

The night, a canvas painted gray,
Where dreams entwine and softly sway.
A dance of souls beneath the veil,
In shadows deep, our whispers sail.

In the stillness, fears release,
In furtive shadows, find our peace.
With every breath, we intertwine,
In this sweet dance, your heart is mine.

## **Traces of Our Softest Moments**

Whispers float on evening air,
Soft glances exchanged with care.
In silence, we find our way,
Moments linger, come what may.

Gentle laughter fills the night,
Hearts twinkle, shared delight.
Hands entwined, a timeless dance,
In your eyes, I see my chance.

Moonlight bathes our woven fate,
In this space, we levitate.
Every heartbeat sings a tune,
Echoes bright as morning's moon.

Old stories stir in quiet dreams,
Wrapped in love's tender seams.
With every touch, we redefine,
The essence of your soul in mine.

As dusk surrenders to the dawn,
In every breath, our love is drawn.
These traces of moments, soft and pure,
A bond that time can never cure.

## A Delicate Exchange of Souls

Your gaze meets mine, a spark ignites,
Silent words dance in moonlit nights.
Every heartbeat sings our song,
In this world, we both belong.

Fingers touch, a fleeting sigh,
In your arms, I learn to fly.
A glance, a nod, a shared embrace,
Two souls find comfort in this space.

Like petals falling from a bloom,
Our spirits rise, dispelling gloom.
The essence of you intertwines,
With whispered hopes and soft designs.

Time stands still, yet quickly flows,
In your laughter, my heart knows.
A delicate exchange takes flight,
Transforming shadows into light.

As twilight deepens into night,
We savor this infinite sight.
Each moment lingers, raw, and true,
In every breath, I'm lost in you.

## The Resonance of Tender Moments

In quiet corners, hearts align,
Whispered dreams, a love divine.
Eyes meet in a knowing glance,
Moments cherished, life's sweet dance.

The sun dips low, colors blend,
Fingers trace as daylight ends.
Every laugh, a gentle wave,
In this rhythm, we both save.

Rustling leaves in softest breeze,
Promises made with such ease.
Time unwinds without a sound,
In your presence, I am found.

Captured in each tender kiss,
In this world, nothing amiss.
The resonance of every sigh,
A melody that won't say goodbye.

As night unfolds its velvet shawl,
We dance together, standing tall.
Every heartbeat writes our tale,
In love's embrace, we shall not fail.

## **Inked in Shared Breath**

Two hearts beat in perfect time,
In every rhythm, a sacred rhyme.
Breath mingles in twilight's glow,
A bond that deepens, love will grow.

With whispered hopes and softest sighs,
Together, we dance beneath the skies.
Sealed in moments, soft and sweet,
In your gaze, my world's complete.

Dreams awaken, new horizons call,
In shared breaths, we embrace it all.
Every laugh, a spark that ignites,
Drawing us closer through starry nights.

Ink stains on our hearts remain,
Tales of joy, and inked with pain.
Yet through it all, we find our way,
In the echoes where memories play.

Forever marked by what we share,
In the silence, we lay bare.
Inked in love, forever blessed,
In this union, we find rest.

## Resonance of the Heartbeat

In silence, she hears a sound,
A rhythm gently pulsing round.
Each beat whispers, soft and clear,
A melody only she can hear.

The night wraps close, a tender shroud,
As echoes rise above the crowd.
In the dark, the pulse will sway,
Guiding her through night and day.

With every thump, a promise made,
Of love that never will degrade.
A song that time cannot dismiss,
A heartbeat that breathes endless bliss.

Through valleys wide and mountains steep,
In memories cherished, forever keep.
Linked by the threads of fate so fine,
Two heartbeats hum, in perfect line.

In softest whispers, secrets flow,
A bond that only they will know.
In every moment, side by side,
The resonance of love, their guide.

## **Memory's Tender Tapestry**

Threads of the past, in colors bright,
Weave through the canvas of soft twilight.
Each stitch a story, woven with care,
A tapestry rich, beyond compare.

The laughter echoes, the tears have dried,
In every pattern, love has tried.
Moments captured, in fibers spun,
A legacy told, of joy and fun.

Hands that once spun, now gently trace,
The memories held in a warm embrace.
Each corner stitched, a tale unfolds,
Of dreams once whispered, now retold.

Sun-kissed days and starry nights,
The tapestry glimmers with soft lights.
In every fold, a heartbeat lives,
In memory's quilt, my spirit gives.

A tapestry woven with threads divine,
Where every color is a lifeline.
In gentle strokes, the past will stay,
Forever cherished, come what may.

## **The Unvoiced Connection**

In quiet corners, glances pass,
No words are spoken, but feelings mass.
A spark ignites in silent air,
Two souls entwined, a dream laid bare.

Through subtle signs, their hearts will know,
The language of love, where whispers flow.
In every sigh, a world begins,
An unvoiced tale, where silence wins.

As shadows merge in twilight's hue,
The bond they share feels tried and true.
No need for words, just souls aligned,
In every moment, their hearts combined.

With every heartbeat, tension builds,
A gentle thrill that love fulfills.
In unspoken words, their truth resides,
The depths of connection, where time abides.

Through whispered dreams in the night sky,
Their spirits soar, unbound, they fly.
In the echoes of a love so bright,
They find their peace in the still of night.

## Chasing Shadows of the Past

In corridors of memory, I roam,
Where shadows dance and dreams call home.
Whispers linger like morning mist,
In echoes of time, I find what's missed.

Chasing fragments of days gone by,
With every step, a silent sigh.
Footsteps soft on familiar ground,
In every turn, lost moments found.

The laughter haunts, the sorrow clings,
To fleeting days when life took wings.
In the twilight glow, I search for light,
Through shadows deep, into the night.

Lessons learnt in the softest grace,
As time unveils each hidden face.
Carried forth by the gentle breeze,
In memory's arms, my heart finds ease.

Yet shadows fade when dawn breaks clear,
Illuminating paths once held dear.
Through the journey, I'll always know,
The beauty lies in what we sow.

## **Whispers Beneath the Stars**

The night is deep and still,
A silver glow alights the hill.
Soft secrets dance on the breeze,
Whispers shared among the trees.

Constellations gleam above,
Each twinkle speaks of love.
Echoes drift through the air,
Stories told in moments rare.

A world alive with quiet dreams,
Moonlit paths and gentle streams.
In shadows cast by starlit grace,
We find our hearts, our sacred place.

With every breath, the night unfolds,
Mysteries of yearning told.
Beneath the stars, we dare to seek,
The whispered truths that hearts now speak.

Together wrapped in silver light,
Lost in wonder, hearts take flight.
In this realm where dreams reside,
Whispers found, no need to hide.

## Notes from the Heart's Diary

In quiet corners of my mind,
I sift through treasures, love defined.
Each note a breath, a tender sigh,
Words that dance and flutter by.

Pages worn from grief and grace,
A tapestry, each thread in place.
Ink spills tales of joy and pain,
In the margins, hope remains.

Memoirs etched in silence deep,
Promises that hearts still keep.
Between the lines, a heartbeat's song,
Each melody where we belong.

The diary whispers, soft and clear,
With every secret, it draws me near.
In the library of the soul,
We find the pieces that make us whole.

So let us write on pages bare,
In twilight's glow, we're free to share.
Notes from the heart, a symphony,
A song of love, our legacy.

## The Unfolding of Desire

In the hush of dawn's embrace,
Desires bloom, a gentle trace.
Petals open, vibrant, new,
Each whisper reveals a clue.

With every heartbeat, sparks ignite,
Fires dance in morning light.
A canvas bright, the colors blend,
A journey where our souls ascend.

In dreams entwined, we lose the past,
Moments fading, shadows cast.
Yet in the yearning, we stand tall,
To rise, to risk, to feel it all.

The tides of passion pull and sway,
An ocean deep, we drift away.
In the rhythm of our hearts' tune,
Desire unfolds, a sweet monsoon.

So let us wander, hand in hand,
Through fields of light, our hearts expand.
In the unfolding, we'll find our way,
Embracing truth, come what may.

## Soft Lanterns in the Dark

Beneath the sky, where shadows play,
Soft lanterns guide our way.
Flickering lights in deep night's fold,
Casting warmth as stories unfold.

With every step, a glow ignites,
Illuminating dreams and nights.
Whispers of hope in gentle flight,
Casting away the creeping fright.

Each lantern holds a spark of fate,
In darkness, we celebrate.
The journey long, yet hearts remain,
By softest light, we'll face the rain.

In the glow of love's embrace,
Every shadow finds its place.
Together we navigate the night,
Soft lanterns shining ever bright.

So, let us wander, spirits free,
Guided by light, just you and me.
In the darkness, we claim our space,
Soft lanterns glow, a warm embrace.

# The Architecture of Understanding

In shadows cast by ancient walls,
We find the echoes of our calls.
Each brick a story, each beam a song,
Crafting a space where we belong.

The arches rise, holding the light,
Whispers of wisdom guide our sight.
In every corner, voices blend,
Building a bridge that knows no end.

With patience, we lay our trust,
As time weaves dreams from dust.
Foundations strong, yet gentle too,
A structure born from me and you.

Each window frames the world outside,
Reflecting hopes we cannot hide.
We craft a vault of shared embrace,
In this arena, love finds space.

And though the storms may test our ground,
In unity, our peace is found.
With every choice, we sketch anew,
The architecture of me and you.

## Meeting in the Silence

In the hush, our breaths align,
Words unspoken, hearts combine.
Moments linger, softly shared,
In stillness, we show we cared.

The world outside may rush and swirl,
Yet here, our gentle whispers twirl.
A sanctuary built on trust,
Our souls connect, a sacred dust.

In silence held, no fear intrudes,
Our spirits dance, the quiet moods.
Time pauses, letting love unfold,
This meeting, worth more than gold.

Together we weave a tapestry,
Every thread a memory.
With every glance, a promise made,
In this silence, we won't fade.

And when the noise begins to swell,
We'll carry our peace, a hidden spell.
In the quiet, we'll always find,
The solace of our intertwined.

## An Unsung Ballad of Us

In gentle tones where shadows play,
We hum a tune of yesterday.
Each note a memory, soft and bright,
A ballad born from shared delight.

Through winding paths our story flows,
In whispered secrets, laughter grows.
Unwritten tales in twilight's gleam,
We sing together, a waking dream.

Though not a crowd will hear our song,
In quiet moments, we belong.
An opus crafted, just for two,
The notes reflect our love so true.

With every sigh and tender glance,
We dance within this sweet romance.
An unsung ballad, soft yet clear,
With every heartbeat, love draws near.

And in the silence, we will know,
The sweetest verses, soft and slow.
In every whisper, every bliss,
Our song endures, a timeless kiss.

## **The Glimmer of Inner Voices**

Within the depths, a spark ignites,
A chorus sings through quiet nights.
Soft murmurs rise, like morning dew,
The glimmering truth of me and you.

From shadows deep, our thoughts take flight,
Guided by dreams that crave the light.
Echoes gather, a symphony,
Each note a glimpse of what can be.

In every heartbeat, whispers dance,
A gentle call, a second chance.
We listen close, with open hearts,
Finding peace as the silence parts.

These voices, wrapped in tender care,
Remind us always love is there.
A glimmer in the darkened space,
A soft embrace, an endless grace.

As daybreak breaks the night's fine thread,
We'll follow where our hearts are led.
In union, let our spirits soar,
The glimmer of us, forevermore.

## **Threads of Unspoken Desire**

In the shadows, whispers stir,
Fingers trace where words are blurred.
Longing lingers in the air,
Silent glances, moments rare.

Tangled thoughts in twilight glow,
Hearts connect, yet fear to show.
Promises dance on fragile lines,
Yearning deep beneath confines.

A touch that sparks electric fire,
Hidden dreams of bold desire.
Threads entwined, a subtle weave,
In the silence, we believe.

Veils of doubt may block the view,
But passion burns, a light so true.
Every heartbeat speaks the past,
In this space, our fate is cast.

We walk a path of quiet grace,
Entwined souls in this sacred space.
Each unspoken word our guide,
In this dance, we cannot hide.

## Caresses in the Quiet

In moonlight's glow, stillness reigns,
Soft whispers course through gentle veins.
Fingers brush with tender care,
In the quiet, love laid bare.

The world outside fades from sight,
As hearts collide in soft twilight.
Every sigh, a sweet refrain,
In silence, we feel no pain.

Hands entwined, the night holds fast,
Moments weave, forever cast.
In the space where shadows play,
Caresses linger, night turns day.

Your breath, a breeze, so soft, so near,
In the quiet, all is clear.
Every heartbeat, every sigh,
In this stillness, we can fly.

Each gaze exchanged, a story spun,
In the quiet, two become one.
Lost in time, no need for sound,
In the silence, love is found.

## **The Vocabulary of Embrace**

In your arms, I learn to speak,
Words unspoken, warmth unique.
Each embrace a story told,
In your grasp, my heart unfolds.

Gentle whispers fill the void,
Love defined, never destroyed.
The language flows, we intertwine,
In every touch, your heart is mine.

Body's rhythm, soft and slow,
Every curve, a place to go.
No need for words, we understand,
In silence, love's command.

The grammar of your quiet sigh
Speaks a truth that will not die.
In the space where lips collide,
We write our vows, side by side.

With each heartbeat, we create,
A lexicon we celebrate.
In this bond, so deep, so vast,
Forever held in love's steadfast.

## **Unraveled Hearts**

Beneath the stars, we share our fears,
Unraveled hearts tell tales through tears.
With every beat, a secret sigh,
Together we learn to fly.

Fragile strings that tie and bind,
In vulnerability, love defined.
Each crack, a glimpse of what we are,
In unity, we'll reach the stars.

Time may fray the edges worn,
But in the night, new hopes are born.
Through tangled paths, we find the light,
To mend our hearts, ignite the night.

Hands that tremble, eyes that glow,
In every heartbeat, love will flow.
Unraveled, yet we stand as one,
In this journey, we have won.

With each embrace, our spirits blend,
In this love, there's no end.
Unraveled yet forever whole,
In each other, we find our soul.

## **The Unseen Bond**

In quiet moments, hearts align,
A pull invisible, yet divine.
Through whispered thoughts and gentle smiles,
We navigate the silent miles.

Like shadowed paths that intertwine,
Two souls, one story, yours and mine.
The world outside may come and go,
But here, a sacred trust will grow.

In laughter shared and tears expressed,
Our spirits dance, forever blessed.
An anchor forged by hopes and dreams,
In unity, we mend the seams.

Though miles apart, we feel it near,
An unseen thread that draws us here.
With every beat, our kinship strong,
In silent songs, we both belong.

Through time and trials, our bond will stand,
A tapestry woven hand in hand.
With love as light, we'll chase the night,
Together, we're a guiding light.

## Inscribed in the Air

Words float lightly, soft as dew,
Carried whispers, me and you.
In silent sighs, our secrets blend,
Promising tales that never end.

Through shadows cast by setting sun,
Our stories rise, two hearts as one.
A tapestry of dreams laid bare,
Each breath we take, inscribed in air.

Unspoken vows, we share in grace,
Mapped out journeys, time can't erase.
In moments lost, we find our way,
The dawn of love in each new day.

Like gentle breezes that kiss the ground,
In quiet spaces, hope is found.
In every glance, our spirits sing,
A promise kept, the joy it brings.

Weathered paths and winding roads,
In the sky, our story glows.
Through every shift, we hold it true,
Inscribed in air, our love anew.

## The Palette of Shared Glances

In fleeting looks, a canvas speaks,
Where colors blend, our vision peaks.
A brush of warmth, a stroke of light,
In simple scenes, the world ignites.

With every glance, emotions flow,
A vibrant dance of ebb and glow.
In shades of laughter, hues of tears,
We paint the moments, calm our fears.

A symphony of silent cues,
The depth of love in varied hues.
Each eye's embrace, a story told,
In vivid tones, our lives unfold.

Through shades of twilight, dusk will blend,
As day departs, our hearts transcend.
The palette shifts, yet love remains,
In every glance, passion sustains.

Together we create, as one,
A masterpiece as bright as sun.
With every look, we shape our fate,
A canvas drawn, never too late.

## Timeless Gestures

In gentle touches, we relate,
Each movement speaks, we resonate.
A simple nod or knowing smile,
In fleeting moments, time feels style.

A heartbeat shared, a sigh, a glance,
In stillness found, our souls do dance.
With every gesture, love we save,
A fleeting path, yet boldly brave.

In shared embraces, warmth unfolds,
An ageless bond, worth more than gold.
Through every silence, sparks remain,
In tender acts, our hearts unchain.

A secret glance across the room,
In crowded spaces, love will bloom.
Through whispered dreams and midnight calls,
Each gesture strengthens, love enthralls.

As time rolls on, our signs endure,
In every hug, our peace is sure.
With timeless gestures, we will find,
A love that's deep, forever kind.

## Muted Melodies of Connection

In a hush, whispers drift low,
Silent chords in twilight glow.
Hearts beat softly, time slips away,
In the calm, we find our sway.

Fingers brush, a brush of fate,
In stillness, we meditate.
Echoes linger, a dance for two,
In each note, a bond so true.

Unseen ties in the space we shape,
In the quiet, our dreams escape.
Language fades, yet blooms anew,
In these muted shades of blue.

Reverberations, gentle and sweet,
In every heartbeat, we repeat.
Strings of laughter, a soft refrain,
In this silence, love's pure gain.

Through the shadows, light will weave,
In this stillness, we believe.
Melodies blend like sunset hues,
In our solitude, we choose.

## The Hearth of Untold Stories

By the fire, old tales arise,
Crackling warmth, beneath the skies.
In the glow, what truths ignite,
Whispers shared in the soft night.

Sparks dance freely, dreams take flight,
In this chamber, hearts unite.
With every flicker, a memory flows,
The hearth, a keeper of love's prose.

Unraveled moments, stitched with care,
In laughter, a story laid bare.
Silent gazes, with words unsaid,
In this glow, our fears are shed.

Tales of old, and futures bright,
In the flames, we find our light.
Each ember carries a soft decree,
In this space, we all can be.

From twilight's hush to morning's song,
At this hearth, we all belong.
Echoes linger in the mind,
In these stories, love entwined.

As shadows dance on wooden floors,
We gather close, amidst the roars.
With each tale, our spirits soar,
In shared moments, we love more.

## **Serendipity in Hand-Holding**


Fingers intertwine, a gentle clasp,
In the midst of chaos, we find the grasp.
Serendipity wrapped in a touch,
In that moment, we feel so much.

Steps align on an unseen path,
In sweet silence, we escape wrath.
The world dissolves in a tender embrace,
In our togetherness, we find grace.

Unearthed laughter in whispers shared,
In this bond, we are unpaired.
Joy unfolds in simple acts,
In this union, no need for facts.

Time suspends in a fleeting glance,
In the intimacy, we find romance.
Every heartbeat, a promise made,
In this dance, our fears will fade.

A journey forged as we two combine,
In this union, pure and divine.
Life's unpredictable twists now seem,
In our hands, we shape the dream.

Amidst the world, we carve a space,
With every squeeze, we find our place.
Serendipity blooms in simple ways,
In hand-holding, our souls blaze.

## The Mute Symphony of Two

In stillness, a symphony unfolds,
With silent whispers, our love molds.
Notes unplayed, yet hearts know well,
In this quiet, sweet stories dwell.

Each glance exchanged speaks a tune,
Under the stars or in afternoons.
Harmony strikes without a sound,
In this fervor, we are unbound.

Chords of memory gently play,
In the shadows, night meets day.
Fingers dance in a sacred space,
In this symphony, time leaves a trace.

The crescendo builds, yet not a cry,
In our silence, we learn to fly.
Breathless moments, two souls as one,
In this music, we come undone.

Cadences flow in a tender hush,
With every heartbeat, feelings brush.
Together we compose, a flawless blend,
In this mute dance, love has no end.

Our symphony swells with light unseen,
In this quiet hush, we glean.
Together we feel, together we sigh,
In this mute symphony, we soar high.

## **The Language of Togetherness**

In whispers soft, our hearts confide,
With every glance, love's secrets glide.
Through laughter's echo, we find our way,
A dance of souls, in light they sway.

In silence shared, we build our trust,
With every promise, a bond robust.
The world outside may spin and churn,
But in this space, our passions burn.

With tender words, our hopes entwine,
A sacred script, your heart and mine.
In moments brief, yet deeply felt,
A tapestry, our feelings melt.

Together we craft, through joy and pain,
Our unity forms a sweet refrain.
With every heartbeat, a pulse divine,
In this language, your hand in mine.

The dawn may break, yet still we stand,
United, steadfast, a timeless band.
In every dream, our visions blend,
The language of love, that will not end.

## **Gentle Rhapsody of Us**

In moonlight's glow, our dreams take flight,
A symphony sung in the hush of night.
With every pulse, a soothing song,
Together, we drift where we belong.

Like rivers flowing, our spirits merge,
In harmony's flow, we gently surge.
With every sigh, a note we share,
In laughter's lilt, love fills the air.

With starlit whispers, we weave delight,
Our moments bathe in the softest light.
As shadows dance, our souls align,
In every heartbeat, your pulse with mine.

In tender glances, the world fades away,
A gentle rhapsody in soft array.
Each memory etched, forever to last,
Embracing the present, entwined with the past.

From dawn's embrace to twilight's sigh,
With open hearts, beneath the sky.
In this melody, forever we'll trust,
A gentle rhapsody, just me and us.

## **Canvases of Hidden Yearnings**

Upon the canvas, dreams take flight,
Colors blend in the soft twilight.
With every stroke, a feeling wakes,
Hidden yearnings in the art we make.

The palette spills with shades of grace,
Emotions linger in every space.
With whispers soft, we paint our tales,
In vibrant hues, where love prevails.

In shadows cast by a gentle hand,
Crafting stories, a silent band.
Each moment glimpsed, a brush's touch,
In every line, we reveal so much.

Through swirling depths, our spirits play,
In every hue, we find our way.
Like whispers wrapped in evening's mist,
These canvases hold the dreams we've kissed.

With every canvas, a chapter drawn,
In colors bright, the endless dawn.
For in this art, our truths reside,
Canvases rich, where hearts collide.

## **Imprints of a Shared Breath**

In stillness held, our souls align,
With every breath, our hearts entwine.
Through fleeting moments, we find our way,
In whispered echoes, love's ballet.

With gentle rhythms, our spirits flow,
In perfect harmony, we come to know.
Each sigh a secret, softly shared,
In this embrace, our souls are bared.

The world may tremble, but we remain,
Imprints of love, through joy and pain.
With every heartbeat, a tale unfolds,
The promise of us, in silence holds.

In twilight's glow, we weave our dreams,
Tracing the light where hope redeems.
With breaths in sync, our futures rise,
The imprints of love beneath the skies.

In every heartbeat, a truth we find,
With every whisper, we're intertwined.
For in this life, where moments blend,
Imprints of a shared breath, without end.

## The Language That Perfectly Listens

In whispers soft, the shadows play,
Silent words that drift away.
Every sigh, a tale untold,
In quiet moments, hearts unfold.

Like raindrops dance on window panes,
Emotions flow through gentle veins.
Eyes that meet with knowing grace,
In silence, we both find our place.

## The Lexicon of Fleeting Touch

Fingers brush like fleeting winds,
In that spark, a magic spins.
A gentle graze, a fleeting sign,
Words unspoken intertwine.

Echoes linger, sweet as night,
In a glance, we take to flight.
Moments pass like sands in glass,
Love's soft language as we pass.

## The Weight of Unexpressed Vows

Promises linger in the air,
Softly spoken, yet so rare.
In the stillness, burdens grow,
Words held back, like quiet snow.

Eyes convey what lips can't share,
In the shadows, hearts lay bare.
Between us, a heavy pause,
The weight of vows without a cause.

## **Dreams Shared in Stillness**

In twilight's hush, our dreams align,
    Softly woven, yours and mine.
Like stars that blink in velvet skies,
Our hopes take flight, in quiet sighs.

Whispers flow like streams at night,
    Together we explore the light.
In stillness thick with softest grace,
We find our dreams, a sacred space.

## **Notes from the Depths of Desire**

In shadows linger thoughts untamed,
Whispers of secrets softly claimed.
Through the night, passion's fire glows,
Yearning's dance in silent throes.

A heart awash in longing's tide,
Searching for solace, nowhere to hide.
With every breath, dreams intertwine,
Elegance found in a lover's design.

Words unspoken fill the air,
An uncharted realm, a silent dare.
In every glance, a story spun,
Desire awakens, forever begun.

Roses and thorns, a tender thread,
A journey crafted, this life we led.
Yet in the depths, we must explore,
A symphony played at a hidden score.

For between the heartbeats, a truth remains,
Mapping the pathways of love's terrains.
In tender notes, let longing find,
The very essence of passions blind.

**Embracing the Unsung**

In quiet corners, the stories rest,
Voices hushed, yet they are blessed.
Each untold tale, a treasure rare,
In shadows, dreams take flight with care.

Fading echoes of lives lived deep,
In corners where memories softly sleep.
Strength resides in the overlooked,
In every glance, a world unhooked.

A gentle sigh upon the breeze,
Whispers of hope in silent pleas.
The unsung heart beats strong and true,
Through every struggle, birth anew.

Casting light on paths less worn,
Nurturing seeds of the unloved, forlorn.
Together we rise, hand in hand,
In harmony's embrace, we understand.

For every shadow hides a glow,
In the unsung, we learn to grow.
A chorus of souls, bold and bright,
In unison, we bring forth the light.

## **Conversations in Quiet Moments**

In stillness shared, our voices blend,
Moments linger, before they end.
Soft-spoken words float in the air,
A symphony found without a care.

Each glance exchanged, a dialogue new,
In the silence, our hearts pursue.
Stories woven on gentle threads,
In whispered dreams, affection spreads.

The clock ticks slow in this sacred space,
Time stands still, a warm embrace.
Every breath forms an unspoken bond,
In tranquil realms, we grow fond.

The sun dips low, casting hues of gold,
In these quiet moments, our truths unfold.
We sip the silence, taste its grace,
In the shadows, we find our place.

For conversations that need no sound,
In the stillness, love is found.
Together, in this serene array,
Our hearts converse, come what may.

## **The Palette of Unexpressed Yearnings**

A canvas blank, yearning's display,
Brushes poised, the hues of gray.
Each stroke a hope, a dream unmet,
In bold colors, we place our debt.

A splash of red for love's sweet plea,
In every shade, we long to be.
The golden hues of laughter's song,
Yet shadows linger, lingering long.

Indigo whispers of distant nights,
Emerald visions twinkling lights.
Each yearning hidden, a tale to tell,
In every layer, we weave our spell.

We dip our brushes into despair,
Painting wishes on canvas bare.
For every sigh, a stroke anew,
In this palette, we dream what's true.

Among the swirls, our hearts collide,
In the depths, our spirits abide.
With each creation, we set free,
The yearning within, our legacy.

## **When Hearts Speak in Verse**

In whispers soft, our hearts converse,
Each pulse and sigh, the language terse.
With every beat, a line unfurls,
A melody where love twirls.

Time freezes still, as starlight beams,
We weave our dreams in moonlit themes.
In perfect rhyme, our souls align,
When hearts confess, the world is fine.

A gentle touch, a glance, a sigh,
The poetry that will not die.
In silent moments, truths emerge,
Our feelings rise like ocean surge.

Through every laugh, through every tear,
The verses grow, they hold us near.
Together we, in rhythm sway,
Our hearts will guide, come what may.

For in this dance, the world will see,
The beauty found in you and me.
When hearts speak soft, in love's embrace,
We pen our tale, a timeless grace.

## The Unraveled Thread of Us

With gentle hands, we weave our fate,
A tapestry that will not wait.
Through laughter shared, and whispers low,
The vibrant colors start to glow.

Yet shadows creep, and threads unwind,
With every truth, new paths we find.
In tangled knots, we stand our ground,
Through every twist, our love profound.

The fragile strands of dreams we chase,
Entwined in time, we find our place.
With every stitch, our hearts persist,
In every hug, a tender tryst.

Though storms may come, and winds may blow,
The love we share still helps us grow.
For in each thread, a story sings,
Of tangled hearts and silver wings.

So let us trace this path ahead,
With every step, so much unsaid.
In all the chaos, love will find,
The strength to bind, the ties that bind.

## **Tender Words on the Wind**

Like petals soft that fall from trees,
Your tender words dance on the breeze.
In quiet moments, pure and bright,
They wrap my heart, a warm delight.

With every breath, your voice I hear,
A symphony that draws me near.
In whispers lost, where dreams take flight,
Our hopes unfold in soft moonlight.

The world outside may fade away,
But in your words, I long to stay.
A world of magic spun from grace,
Where all our fears cannot erase.

With every sigh, a promise made,
In every glance, love's serenade.
Your tender whispers softly blend,
The sweetest tunes that never end.

So let the breeze carry our song,
In every note, where we belong.
Those tender words like feathered flight,
Will be our guide, through day and night.

## **Secrets Written in Softness**

In quiet corners, secrets lie,
Soft whispers dance, they never die.
With gentle grace, we share our fears,
In hidden smiles and unshed tears.

Each word a secret, softly stitched,
In hearts entwined, the light is rich.
Through veils of love, our truths confide,
In tender moments, side by side.

The shadows play, but love remains,
In every heartbeat, joy sustains.
Together we, in silence, trust,
In every hush, a bond robust.

For in our hearts, the stories grow,
Of quiet paths and dreams aglow.
In secret corners, we find peace,
In softness shared, our hearts release.

With every secret, stronger yet,
The bonds we share, we won't forget.
In whispered love, our spirits soar,
As secrets written, forevermore.

Milton Keynes UK
Ingram Content Group UK Ltd.
UKHW022049111124
451035UK00014B/1028

9 789916 866542